INDIAN

the fragrance and foodways
of the Indian ritual for

creative cooking

REBO
PUBLISHERS

Foreword

India is an animated palette of colors, aromas, and impressions. In this vast
and varied country, each region has its own language, customs, tastes,
and cooking styles. The British introduced Indian curry to Europe, but there is so
much more to Indian food than that. Examples of recipes in this book include Dhal
Shorva (lentil soup), Potato Naan Bread, Chicken Rogan Josh, and Lamb Pilaf with
Yogurt. You should certainly try the Masala Duck Curry, and indulge yourself with
Gulab Jamun, a heavenly dessert. In India, the communal meal is always a special
occasion. Eating together stands for harmony, love, and togetherness.

INDIAN

Colophon

© 2003 Rebo International b.v., Lisse, The Netherlands

www.rebo-publishers.com – info@rebo-publishers.com

This 3rd edition reprinted 2004

Original recipes and photographs: © R&R Publishing Pty. Ltd.

Design, editing and production: Minkowsky Graphics, Enkhuizen, The Netherlands

Translation and adaptation: American Pie, London, UK and Sunnyvale, California, USA

ISBN 90 366 1470 8

Abbreviations

tbsp = tablespoon

tsp = teaspoon

g = gram

kg = kilogram

fl oz = fluid ounce

lb = pound

oz = ounce

ml = milliliter

l = liter

°C = degree Celsius

°F = degree Fahrenheit

Where three measurements are given, the first is the American

liquid measure.

Method

1. Heat the oil in a large saucepan. Fry the onion and ginger for 5 minutes or until softened. Add the potatoes and fry for another minute, stirring often.

2. Mix the cumin, coriander, turmeric, and cinnamon with 2 tbsp of cold water to make a paste. Add to the onion and potato, stirring well, and fry for 1 minute to release the flavors.

3. Add the broth and season to taste. Bring to the boil, then reduce the heat, cover, and simmer for 30 minutes or until the potato is tender. Blend until smooth in a food processor or press through a metal sieve. Return to the pan and heat through on low heat. Garnish with the yogurt and sprinkle with more black pepper.

Indian Spices, Potato and Onion Soup

Ingredients

1 tbsp/15ml vegetable oil

1 onion, minced

½in/1cm piece fresh root ginger, finely chopped

2 large potatoes, cut into ½in/1cm cubes

2 tsp/10g ground cumin

2 tsp/10g ground coriander

½ tsp/2.5g turmeric, 1 tsp/5g ground cinnamon

4 cups/1¾ pints/1 l chicken broth

salt and black pepper

1 tbsp/15ml plain yogurt to garnish

Method

1. Heat a dry frying pan, then add the cumin seeds and nigella seeds and toss around the hot pan until they smell roasted and start to crackle, about 3 minutes. Remove the seeds and set them aside.

2. Add the ghee or butter to the pan. Add the finely sliced green onions (scallions) and mint leaves and sauté for a few minutes or until the green onions have wilted.

3. Add the cumin, turmeric, and cashew nuts, and toss until the spices are fragrant and the nuts are golden. Add the drained chickpeas and cook for a further 2 minutes. Set aside.

4. In a mixing bowl, whisk together the yogurt, sour cream, and water until smooth. Season to taste with salt and pepper. Peel the cucumbers and scrape out the seeds. Cut the cucumber flesh into thin slices and add to the yogurt mixture.

5. Add the green-onion-and-spice mixture and sugar to the yogurt and stir thoroughly to combine. Allow the flavors to blend for 1 hour before serving.

6. Garnish with toasted shredded, unsweetened coconut, sliced mint leaves, and a few nigella seeds.

Ingredients

1tsp/5g cumin seeds

1tsp/5g nigella (black onion) seeds

1 tbsp/15ml ghee or butter

4 green onions (scallions), finely sliced

10 fresh mint leaves

2 tsp/10g ground cumin

1tsp/5g turmeric

60g cashew nuts

1¼ cups/10oz/300g can chickpeas, drained and rinsed

Cool Cumin-scented Yogurt Soup

2 cups/16 fl oz/500g plain low fat yogurt

1 scant cup/7fl oz/200ml sour cream

1 scant cup/7fl oz/200ml water

salt and pepper to taste

21/4 cups/1lb 5 oz/ 600g cucumbers

1 tbsp/15g sugar

2 tbsp/30g shredded coconut, toasted

mint leaves for garnish

Indian

Method

First, mix the yogurt with the boiling water and stir well. Set aside for 5 minutes. Mix the all-purpose flour with 1 cup/4oz/125g of the whole-wheat flour and add the yeast. Add the yogurt mixture and stir with a wooden spoon for 3 minutes then allow this yeast sponge to rest for 30 minutes. Add the salt, sugar, oil, and black sesame seeds and enough of the remaining flour to form a firm but moist dough. Begin to knead on a floured surface and continue until the dough is silky and elastic. Allow the dough to rest in an oiled bowl for 1 hour or until doubled in bulk. Meanwhile, make the potato filling. Peel and dice the potatoes and boil in water to cover until soft. Mix the hot potato with the onion, mint leaves, parsley, coriander, cumin, and turmeric. Season to taste with salt and pepper and mash until soft but not sloppy. Cool. Punch down the dough and divide into 12 equal pieces. Roll each out to a circle about 4–6in/10–15cm in diameter. Preheat the oven to 390°F/200°C. Place 1 tbsp/15g of filling in the center and lift both edges of the circle to seal. Pinch the seam together very well. Allow to rise for 10 minutes then brush with beaten egg. Bake for 15–20 minutes or until golden and crisp. Serve on their own or with a tomato relish or herb yogurt dip. Note: For a milder onion flavor in the filling, sauté the onions lightly before adding them to the potato. For more heat, add a little chili pepper to the filling.

Potato Naan Bread

Ingredients

1 cup/8fl oz/250ml plain whole milk yogurt	**Filling**
1½ cups/12fl oz/350ml boiling water	1lb/500g potatoes
2 cups/8 oz/250g all-purpose flour	1 onion, minced
3 cups/12oz/350g whole-wheat flour	4 mint leaves, finely sliced
1 tbsp/15g fresh yeast, 2 tsp/10g salt	¼ cup/2oz/60g chopped parsley½ cup coriander
1tsp/5g sugar	¼ tsp/1.25g cumin
2 tbsp/50ml peanut or walnut oil, 1 egg, beaten	¼ tsp/1.25g turmeric
3 tbsp/45g black sesame seeds	salt and pepper, to taste

Method:

1. Heat the oil in a large saucepan over a medium heat. Add onions, apple, and garlic and cook, stirring, for 5 minutes or until onions are tender. Add lemon juice, curry powder, sugar, cumin, and coriander and cook over a low heat, stirring, for 10 minutes or until fragrant.

2. Blend flour with a little broth and stir into curry mixture. Add chicken, rice, and remaining broth to pan and bring to the boil, stirring constantly. Reduce heat, cover, and simmer for 20 minutes or until chicken and rice are cooked. Season to taste with black pepper.

Mulligatawny Soup

Ingredients

1 tbsp/15ml vegetable oil

2 onions, chopped

1 green apple, cored, peeled, and chopped

1 clove garlic, crushed

2 tbsp/30ml lemon juice

1 tbsp/15g curry powder

1tsp/5g brown sugar

½tsp/2.5g ground cumin

¼tsp/1.25g ground coriander

2 tbsp/15g flour.

8 cups/3½ pints/2l chicken broth

1 lb/500g boneless chicken breast or thigh fillets, cut into ½in/1cm cubes

⅓ cup/2½oz/75g rice

freshly ground black pepper

Note:

A dash of hot pepper sauce, such as Tabasco, and a chopped tomato

are delicious additions to this soup. Serve with crusty bread rolls,

naan, or pita bread.

Method

Pick over the chickpeas and remove any that are discolored. Place all remaining chickpeas in a large saucepan and cover with cold water. Peel 2 of the onions and chop in half. Place these in the saucepan with the chickpeas. Add the cloves and bayleaves, and bring to the boil. Simmer for 10 minutes then remove the chickpeas from the heat and cover and leave for 2 hours to steep. Strain the chickpeas discarding the onions, cloves, and bayleaves, but reserving some of the soaking water.

Chop the remaining 2 onions. Heat the oil and sauté the onions and the minced garlic. Add all the spices and cook briefly to release their fragrance. Add the soaked chickpeas and 2 cups/16 fl oz/500ml of the soaking water, the tomato paste, and the bell pepper strips.

Cover and simmer gently for about 20 minutes until the chickpeas soften and the liquid evaporates. Add the zucchini and salt and pepper to taste. Stir well, then remove from the heat. Allow to cool slightly then fold the spinach leaves into the mixture.

Allow to cool completely before serving.

Ingredients

2 cups/1lb/450g dry chickpeas

4 onions

1tsp/5g whole cloves

4 bayleaves

¼ cup /2 fl oz/60ml peanut or olive oil

4 cloves garlic

1tsp/5g turmeric

Tip

Never add salt to pulses (dried peas and beans) until after the initial cooking or soaking because the salt will toughen the skins and inhibit their ability to absorb liquid.

Indian Chickpea Salad with Spinach

2 tsp/10g cumin

2 tsp/10g garam masala

3 tbsp/45ml tomato paste

2 red bell peppers, sliced

4 medium zucchini (courgettes), sliced on the diagonal

salt and pepper to taste

8 cups/1lb/500g baby leaf spinach

Method

1. Sift the flour and salt into a bowl. Make a well in the center and add the water, a little at a time, using your fingers to incorporate the surrounding flour to make a smooth pliable dough.

2. Knead dough on a lightly floured surface for 5–10 minutes, then place in a bowl, cover with a cloth, and leave for 30–60 minutes.

3. Knead dough for 2–3 minutes. Divide into 6 balls of equal size, then flatten each ball to a circle, about 5in/12.5cm in diameter.

4. Heat an ungreased griddle or electric frying pan until hot. Place one chapatti at a time on the hot surface. As soon as bubbles appear on the surface, turn the chapatti over. Press down on the chapatti with a thick cloth so that it cooks evenly.

5. To finish the chapatti, lift it with a metal spatula and hold it carefully over an open flame without turning until it puffs up slightly or place the chapatti under a hot broiler.

6. Repeat with the remaining dough. Keep the cooked chapattis warm in a covered, napkin-lined basket.

Chapattis

Ingredients

2 cups/8oz/250g whole-wheat flour

1tsp/5g salt

1 cup/7–8fl oz/215–250ml water

Method

In a large saucepan, heat the ghee and add the dahl, mustard seeds, ground coriander, ground cumin, turmeric, cinnamon stick, garlic, minced ginger, curry leaves, onion, and green chili pepper. Cook over a low heat for 5 minutes until the spices are aromatic and deep brown in color and the onion has softened.

Add the vegetable broth and simmer until the dahl is soft, about 30–45 minutes. Remove the cinnamon stick, green chili pepper, and curry leaves.

Blend the dahl until smooth with a hand-held electric beater, then return to the saucepan.

Add the diced vegetables and simmer for a further 20 minutes or until the vegetables are soft.

Add the lemon juice, salt to taste, and chopped coriander. Stir well and serve with a dollop of yogurt, garnished with a few extra coriander leaves.

Ingredients

2 tbsp/30ml ghee or vegetable oil

1½ cups/12oz/350g dahl (yellow or red lentils)

1 tsp/5g mustard seeds

1 tsp/5g ground coriander

1tsp/5g ground cumin, 1½ tsp/7.5g turmeric

1 cinnamon stick, 6 cloves garlic, minced

1 tbsp/15g minced ginger

10 fresh curry leaves, bruised and tied together

1 large onion, finely chopped

Indian Dahl Shorva – Lentil Soup

1 large green chili pepper, whole but split

8 cups/3½ pints/2 l rich vegetable broth

2 tomatoes, finely diced

1 small eggplant, finely diced

1 small carrot, finely diced

1 large potato, peeled and diced

juice of 4 lemons

salt to taste

1 cup/4oz/125g fresh coriander (cilantro) leaves

4 tbsp/60ml plain yogurt

Indian

Method

1. To make the batter, put all the ingredients into a bowl, then gradually add 1 cup/8fl oz/225 ml of water, stirring constantly until combined. Add the shallots, zucchini (courgettes) and eggplant (aubergine) to the batter, mixing well.

2. Pour the oil into a wok to a depth of 2in/5cm and heat over a medium-to-high heat. Check the oil is hot enough by dropping in a small piece of vegetable; it should sizzle. Gently place 4 balls of the mixture (about 2 tbsp/30g each) into the hot oil and fry for 2–3 minutes, until golden. Turn over and cook for a further 2–3 minutes, until crisp.

3. Remove the bhajis with a slotted spoon and drain on kitchen towels. Fry the remaining bhajis in the same way.

Vegetable Bhajis

Ingredients

10 shallots, finely chopped

2 zucchini (courgettes), coarsely grated

1 eggplant (aubergine), finely diced

Vegetable oil for frying

For the batter

¾ cup/3½oz/100g gram (chickpea) flour

¼ cup/2oz/50g ground rice

¼ tsp/1.25g baking soda

1 tsp/5g chili powder

1 tsp/5g turmeric

1-2 tbsp/15-30g curry powder (mild or hot according to taste)

1 tsp/5g salt

Method

In a blender or food processor, grind the corn and salt together until it is finely puréed.

Transfer the mixture to a mixing bowl and add the coriander. Add the flour, a little at a time, continuing until the mixture is kneadable (it should be slightly sticky). Divide the dough into 12 then roll each piece out to a circle about 6in/10–15cm in diameter. If still sticky, use extra all-purpose flour to absorb the moisture. Once rolled, brush each bread with a little ghee.

Heat a griddle or frying pan and add a little ghee to it. Add one bread and cook until the underside is set and spotted with brown. Turn over and cook the other side. Remove the cooked bread and keep warm in foil while cooking the other breads the same way.

If you would like to duplicate the smoky roasted flavor that these breads would have when cooked over an open fire, simply hold each bread over a gas flame for a few seconds, but do not burn. Brush with more ghee and serve.

Ingredients

1 cup/8oz/250g fresh corn kernels

½ tsp/2.5g salt

2 tbsp/30g chopped coriander (cilantro) leaves

1⅓ cups/5oz/150g all-purpose flour

1–2 tbsp ghee (clarified butter), melted

extra flour for dusting and ghee for serving

Indian Fresh Cornbread

Indian

Method

1. To make the spice mixture, place cumin, coriander, mango powder, and turmeric in a small bowl. Stir well and set aside.

2. Boil or microwave the peas and carrots, separately, until just cooked. Drain, refresh under cold running water, and set aside. Heat oil in a heavy-based saucepan over a low heat. Add cumin seeds, ginger, and chili peppers and cook, stirring, for 2–3 minutes. Add peas and carrots and mix well to combine. Stir in the water and salt to taste and simmer for 5 minutes. Add spice mixture and simmer, stirring occasionally, for 5 minutes longer.

To microwave: Place peas, carrots, oil, cumin seeds, ginger, chili peppers, and spice mixture in a microwave-safe dish. Cover and cook on medium (70%), stirring occasionally, for 20 minutes. Season to taste with salt.

Spiced Peas and Carrots

Ingredients

2 cups/8oz/250g frozen or shelled peas

2 carrots, diced

2 tbsp/30ml vegetable oil

1tsp/5g cumin seeds

2 tsp/20g finely chopped fresh ginger

2 red or green chili peppers, finely chopped

5–6 tbsp/75–90ml water, salt

Dry spice mixture:

½ tsp/2.5g ground cumin

¼tsp/1.25g ground coriander

¼tsp/1.25g mango powder

¼tsp/1.25g ground turmeric

Method

Preheat the oven to 350°F/180°C. Generously butter 2 nonstick 6-cup muffin pans.

In a large bowl, combine the flour, baking powder, baking soda, and ground cardamom. Set aside.

Using an electric mixer, cream the butter, sugar, and orange zest together until light and fluffy. Add the eggs and yogurt, and mix on low speed until the ingredients are well combined, then fold the flour mixture in by hand. Do not over-mix.

Divide the batter evenly among the muffin cups and bake for 15–18 minutes. Meanwhile, whisk together the fresh orange juice, marmalade, boiling water, and extra 2 tbsp/50g sugar.

When the orange cakes are baked, remove them from the oven, and loosen the cakes in the muffin cups by running round them with a knife. Spoon the orange syrup over the cakes and allow them to cool in the pans.

Meanwhile, make the sauce. Combine the sugar and water and stir until the sugar has dissolved. Increase the heat and boil vigorously, washing down the sides of the pan with a pastry brush dipped in cold water to prevent crystallization. Continue boiling until the syrup turns a rich, deep gold, then remove the pan from the heat. Carefully add the orange juice to the syrup (be careful because it will splatter). Swirl the pan to dissolve the juice, returning the pan to the heat if necessary. Once the mixture is smooth, remove from the heat and set aside to cool. When cool, whisk in the cream then chill the sauce.

To serve, turn out the cakes and place each on a plate, heap the orange segments on top of the cakes, then spoon the sauce all around.

Ingredients:

For the Cakes:

2 cups/8 oz/250g all-purpose flour

1½ tsp/7.5g baking powder

1tsp/5g baking soda

2 tsp/10g ground cardamom

½ cup/125ml butter, softened

1 cup/8oz/250g sugar

2 oranges, rind grated, juice squeezed

2 large eggs

⅔ cup/5 fl oz/150ml yogurt

2 tbsp/30g sugar

3 tbsp/45ml marmalade

2 tbsp/30ml boiling water

Orange Cardamom Cakes

For the Orange Sauce:

2 cups/1 lb/450g sugar

1 cup/8 fl oz/250ml water

2 oranges, juice squeezed

2 tbsp/30ml heavy (thick) cream

4 large oranges, segmented

Method

First, mix the yogurt with the boiling water and stir well. Set aside for 5 minutes.

Mix the all-purpose flour with 1 cup/4oz/125g of the whole-wheat flour and add the yeast. Add the yogurt mixture and stir with a wooden spoon for 3 minutes then cover with plastic wrap. Leave this yeast sponge to rest for 1 hour to allow the flavors to develop.

Add the salt, sugar, oil, and black sesame seeds and enough of the remaining flour to the sponge to form a firm but moist dough. Begin to knead on a floured surface and continue until the dough is very silky and elastic. Allow the dough to rise in an oiled bowl for 1 hour or until doubled.

Punch down the dough and divide into 8 pieces. Shape each into a ball then flatten each piece of dough into a circle about ⅓in/1cm thick and transfer to oiled cookie sheets.

Brush the surface of the dough with water and sprinkle the surface generously with sesame seeds. With a blade or sharp knife, score the dough from the center to the edge to look like sunrays.

Cover the dough and allow to rise for 10 minutes. Bake on oiled cookie sheets

Naan Bread

Ingredients

1 cup/8 fl oz/250ml plain whole milk yogurt

1½ cups/12 fl oz/350ml boiling water

2 cups/8oz/250g all-purpose (plain) flour

3 cups/12oz/350g whole-wheat flour

1 tbsp/15ml yeast

2 tsp/10g salt

1tsp/5g sugar

2 tbsp30ml peanut oil

3 tbsp/45g black sesame seeds

6 tbsp/90g white sesame seeds

Tip

The naan bread can be topped with other seed

mixtures, including nigella, cardamom, etc.

Method

1. Place onions in a food processor or blender and process to make a purée.

2. Heat oil in a heavy-based saucepan. Add garlic, chili peppers, ginger, cumin seeds, bayleaves, salt to taste, and the onion purée. Cook over a medium heat until the onions are a pinkish color. Add tomatoes, ground cumin, coriander, cloves, cinnamon, cardamom, mango powder, and turmeric and cook, stirring, for 3–4 minutes. Remove pan from heat and stir in cream.

3. Pre-heat oven to 350°F/180°C. Place fish in a baking dish, pour the sauce over it, and bake for 20 minutes or until fish flakes when tested with a fork. Just prior to serving, sprinkle with basil.

Ingredients

	salt
2 large onions, roughly chopped	4 large tomatoes, finely chopped
1 tbsp/15ml vegetable oil	½tsp/2.5g ground cumin
2 cloves garlic, crushed	½tsp/1.5g ground coriander
2 fresh red or green chili peppers, finely chopped	pinch ground cloves
	pinch ground cinnamon
2 tsp/10g finely chopped fresh ginger	pinch ground cardamom
1 tbsp/15g cumin seeds	½ tsp/2.5g mango powder
2 bayleaves	¼ tsp/1.25g ground turmeric

Baked Fish

3 tbsp/45ml heavy (double) cream

4 firm white fish fillets, such as sea-bream or ocean perch

1 bunch fresh basil, leaves removed and finely chopped

Method

1. Sift flour and salt into a bowl. Rub in the butter, then mix in enough water to form a pliable dough. Knead for 10 minutes, then set aside.

2. To make the filling, melt the butter in a frying pan. Add onion, garlic, chili peppers, and ginger and fry for 5–7 minutes, or until onion is golden.

3. Stir in turmeric and chili powder, then add meat and salt. Fry, stirring, until meat is cooked and mixture is fairly dry. Stir in garam masala and lemon juice; cook for 5 minutes more. Remove pan from heat and allow to cool.

4. Divide dough into 15 balls. Flatten each ball and roll out to a paper-thin circle about 4in/10cm in diameter. Dampen the edges of each circle with water and shape into cones. Fill each cone with filling, then pinch them securely together to seal.

5. Deep fry samosas in batches in hot oil for 2–3 minutes or until golden-brown. Drain on paper towels and serve.

Samosas

Ingredients

2 cups/8oz/250g plain flour

½ tsp/1.25g salt

2 tbsp/1oz/30g butter

4–6 tbsp water

Filling:

1oz/30g butter

1 onion, finely chopped

2 cloves garlic, crushed

2 green chili peppers, seeded and chopped

1in/2.5cm piece of fresh root ginger, grated

½ tsp/2.5g ground turmeric

½ tsp/2.5g hot chili powder

1½ cups/12oz /375g lean minced beef or lamb

1 tsp/5g salt

2 tsp/10g Garam Masala (page 15)

juice of ½ lemon

oil for deep frying

Variation:

1. For a vegetarian samosa, make the filling by frying 1 small chopped onion and 1tsp/5g grated fresh root ginger in 1 tbsp/5ml ghee until soft.

2. Stir in 12oz/375g cold mashed potato, 2 tsp/10g garam masala and 1 tbsp/15ml mango chutney (with any large chunks finely chopped). Cook over moderate heat until mixture is fairly dry, then cool. Substitute for the meat filling in the main recipe.

Indian

Method

1. Heat the oil in a heavy-based saucepan over moderately high heat. Add mustard seeds. As soon as they pop, stir in chili powder and asa fœtida. Shake pan briefly over the heat, then add cauliflower flowerets and peas.

2. Stir-fry, for a few seconds, then add potato cubes, tomatoes, turmeric, garam masala, salt, coriander, and molasses.

3. Stir well, cover, and cook for 3–4 minutes, then add measured water, mixing thoroughly. Reduce the heat, cover, and simmer for about 30 minutes or until vegetables are tender and sauce has thickened slightly.

4. Serve hot with Indian flatbreads (puris or chapattis).

Ingredients

2 tbsp/30ml oil

1tsp/5g mustard seeds

½ tsp/2.5g hot chili powder

pinch of asafoetida (hing)

1 cauliflower, divided into flowerets

½ cup/4oz/125g fresh or thawed frozen peas

1 potato, cut into ½in/1cm cubes

2 tomatoes, peeled and finely chopped

½ tsp/2.5g ground turmeric

½ tsp/2.5g garam masala

pinch of salt

Cauliflower and Peas in Chili Sauce

1 tbsp/15g chopped fresh coriander

1 tsp/5ml molasses

1¾ cups/14fl oz/440ml water

Indian

Method:

1. Place split peas in a large bowl, cover with water, stir in baking soda, and set aside to soak overnight.

2. Rinse split peas under cold running water and drain thoroughly. Set aside for at least 30 minutes, then spread out on absorbent kitchen paper to dry. Heat about 2in/5cm oil in a frying pan and cook split peas in batches until golden. Using a slotted spoon, remove peas and drain on absorbent kitchen paper.

3. Transfer cooked peas to a dish, sprinkle with chili powder, coriander, cinnamon, cloves, and salt and toss to coat. Allow peas to cool and store in an airtight container.

Crunchy Split Peas

Ingredients

¾ cup/6oz/185g yellow split peas or a mixture
of yellow split peas and green split peas

2 tsp/10g baking soda

oil for deep-frying

½ tsp/2.5g chili powder

½ tsp/2.5g ground coriander

pinch ground cinnamon

pinch ground cloves

1 tsp/5g salt

Method

Mix the whole-wheat flour, all-purpose flour, salt, and coconut in a bowl with the chili powder and sugar. Add the melted ghee or oil and rub through until the flour appears crumbly. Add the water, stirring while adding only as much as is needed to form a soft dough. Knead the dough well then allow it to rest for 10 minutes.

Divide the dough into 14 pieces, flattening them and rolling them out to thin circles of 3in/8cm in diameter.

Heat the oil in a wok and, when hot, add one bread. Use a metal skimmer or spatula to push the bread under the oil until it is puffed and golden. Allow the bread to float, turning to cook the other side.

Drain on absorbent paper and cook the other pooris the same way.

Note:

Although it is important not to overcrowd the wok, which would reduce the temperature of the oil and make the pooris soggy, 3 or 4 poori can usually be cooked together.

Ingredients

2 scant cups/7oz/200g whole-wheat flour or Indian atta flour

⅔ cup/3½oz/100g all-purpose flour

½–1 tsp/2.5–5g salt

⅔ cup/3½oz/100g shredded unsweetened coconut

1 tsp/5g chili powder

½ tbsp/2.5g sugar

Coconut Poori

2 tbsp/30ml ghee (clarified butter) or vegetable oil

⅔ cup/5oz/150ml water, approximately

oil for frying

Indian

Method

Rinse the rice well in a sieve under running water. Bring 4 cups/1¾ pints/1 l of water to the boil, and add salt and lemon juice. Stir in the rice and, when water returns to the boil, reduce the heat and simmer for 18 minutes or until rice is just tender. Drain in colander and rinse with hot water. Set aside.

Heat ghee in a large frying pan. Add onion and cook until transparent. Add cashews and yellow raisins, and sauté a little for 3 minutes. Add spices and 1 tsp/5ml of ghee and cook, stirring constantly, for 2 minutes.

Add drained rice, gently toss to combine ingredients, and reheat the rice. Serve hot with curries or as a side-dish with broiled meats and chicken.

Ingredients

1½ cups/12 oz/350g basmati (long-grain) rice

4 cups/1¾ pints/1 l water

½ tsp/2.5g salt

2 tbsp/30ml lemon juice

2 tbsp/30ml ghee

1 medium Bermuda onion, chopped

3 tbsp/45g cashew nuts

Spiced Rice

3 tbsp/45g yellow raisins

¼ tsp/1.25g fennel seeds

¼ tsp/1.25g cumin seeds

¼ tsp/1.25g white mustard seeds

¼ tsp/1.25g ground turmeric

1 tsp/5g ghee plus extra for serving

Indian

Method

1. Briefly grind the saffron using a pestle and mortar, then mix the powder with 1 tbsp/15ml boiling water and set aside. Rinse the rice and drain.

2. Melt the butter in a large, heavy-based saucepan. Fry the shallot gently for 2 minutes or until softened. Add the cardamom pods, cinnamon, and rice, and mix well.

3. Add 1¼ cups10 fl oz/300ml of water, the saffron mixture, and salt. Bring to the boil, then reduce the heat and cover the pan tightly. Simmer the rice for 15 minutes or until the liquid has been absorbed and the rice is tender. Discard the cardamom pods and cinnamon stick before serving.

Fragrant Pilau Rice

Ingredients

large pinch of saffron strands

1 cup/8oz/225g basmati rice

2 tbsp/1oz/25g butter

1 shallot, minced

3 cardamom pods

1 cinnamon stick

salt

Method

Bring 6 cups/2½ pints/1½ l of the vegetable broth to the boil and add the lentils.

Simmer until the lentils are tender, but still retain their shape, about 20 minutes.

Drain well, then transfer the lentils to a large bowl. Add the lemon juice

and 1 tbsp/15ml of the oil. Mix well, cover, and chill.

Combine the curry powder, garam masala, and turmeric in a plastic bag with salt

and pepper to taste, then add the chicken breasts to the bag. Seal the bag

and shake vigorously, allowing the spices to coat the chicken breasts evenly. Heat

a broiler pan or nonstick frying pan. Add the remaining oil and heat until smoking,

then add the chicken breasts to the pan. Cook until golden brown and cooked

through on both sides, about 5 minutes. Remove the chicken and set aside.

To the used pan, add the remaining broth and bring to the boil. Add the cauliflower

and peas and cook over high heat until vegetables are crisp-tender and most

of liquid has evaporated, about 5 minutes. Add this vegetable mixture to the lentils

and mix well. Add the diced tomatoes, diced cucumber, sliced green onions

(scallions), and chopped fresh mint, and mix well, adding salt and pepper to taste.

Slice the chicken into diagonal strips then gently fold these into the salad. Arrange

the watercress on a serving platter and top with the salad mixture, arranging so that

plenty of chicken is visible. Garnish with fresh mint and green onions (scallions).

Ingredients

7½ cups/3 pints/1.75 l vegetable broth

1½ cups/12oz/350g dried lentils

2 lemons, juice squeezed

5 tsp/1⅓oz/40ml vegetable oil

1 tbsp/15g curry powder

1 tbsp/15g garam masala

1 tsp/5g turmeric

salt and pepper to taste

4 large chicken breast fillets, skin removed

1 small cauliflower, cut into flowerets

1½ cups/12oz/350g fresh or frozen peas

2 small tomatoes, seeded, diced

1 cucumber, peeled and diced

2 green onions (scallions), sliced

2 tbsp/10g chopped fresh mint

Spiced Chicken and Dahl Salad

salt and pepper to taste

2 large bunches watercress, trimmed

fresh mint, extra, for garnish

green onions (scallions), for garnish

Indian

Method

1. Heat oil in a Dutch oven (casserole), add onion and fry for 5–7 minutes, stirring frequently, until browned but not crisp.

2. Stir in turmeric, cumin seeds, ginger, and chili pepper, then add potatoes and cook gently for 5 minutes, stirring frequently.

3. Stir in peas. Cover casserole and simmer over very low heat for 15–20 minutes or until potatoes are tender but retain their shape. Garnish and serve.

Potato and Pea Bhajee

Ingredients

3–4 tbsp oil

1 onion, thinly sliced

1 tsp/5g ground turmeric

1 tsp/5g cumin seeds

¼ tsp/1.25g ground ginger

1 green chili pepper, seeded and chopped

4 cups/1 lb/500g potatoes, peeled and diced

1 cup/8oz/250g fresh or thawed frozen peas

chopped fresh coriander to garnish

Method:

1. Melt ghee or butter in a saucepan over a medium heat, add garlic and onions and cook, stirring, for 3 minutes, or until onions are golden.

2. Stir in curry paste, coriander, and nutmeg, and cook for 2 minutes or until fragrant.

Add chicken and cook, stirring, for 5 minutes or until chicken is brown.

3. Add cashews, cream, and coconut milk. Bring to the boil and simmer, stirring occasionally, for 40 minutes or until chicken is tender.

To toast the cashews, spread nuts over a cookie sheet and bake at 350°F/180°C for 5–10 minutes or until lightly and evenly browned. Toss back and forth occasionally with a spoon to ensure even browning. Alternatively, place nuts under a medium broiler and cook, tossing back and forth until toasted.

Ingredients

4 tbsp/2oz/60g ghee or butter

2 cloves garlic, crushed

2 onions, minced

1 tbsp/15g curry paste

1 tbsp/15g ground coriander

½ tsp/2.5g ground nutmeg

Cashew Nut Butter Chicken

1½ lb/750g boneless chicken thigh or breast fillets,

cut into ¾ in/2cm cubes

2oz/60g cashews, roasted and ground

1¼ cups/10fl oz/315ml heavy (double) cream

2 tbsp/30ml coconut milk

Indian

Method

1. Heat ghee in a large frying pan and cook onions for 2–3 minutes or until golden brown. Remove from pan and set aside.

2. Add chicken to the pan and cook until well browned on all sides. Remove from pan and set aside.

3. Combine ginger, garlic, cumin, cinnamon, cloves, cardamom, nutmeg, and flour. Stir into pan and cook for 1–2 minutes. Add broth, yogurt, and cream, stirring and scraping the bottom of the pan.

4. Return chicken to the pan with half the onions. Cover and simmer for 15–20 minutes. Remove from heat and stand, covered, for 15 minutes.

5. To make rice pilau, heat ghee in a large saucepan. Cook saffron, cardamom, salt, and rice for 1–2 minutes. Pour in broth and bring to the boil. Add yellow raisins, reduce heat, and cook gently for 10–15 minutes or until most of the broth is absorbed. Cover and set aside for 10 minutes. Preheat oven to 350°F/180°C.

6. Transfer half the rice to a large ovenproof dish, top with chicken pieces, then remaining rice. Drizzle over sauce from chicken, top with remaining onions and cashew nuts. Cover and bake in the oven for 20–30 minutes.

Ingredients

3 tbsp/45g ghee

3 onions, sliced

3 lb/1½kg chicken pieces

2 tsp/10g grated fresh ginger

3 cloves garlic, crushed

½ tsp/2.5g ground cumin

½ tsp/2.5g ground cinnamon

¼ tsp/1.25g ground cloves

¼ tsp/1.25g ground cardamom

¼ tsp/1.25g ground nutmeg

2 tsp/5g all-purpose flour

1 cup/8 fl oz/250ml chicken broth

½ cup/4fl oz/125ml plain yogurt

½ cup/4fl oz/125ml light (single) cream

Chicken Biryani

Rice Pilau:

2 tbsp/30ml ghee

½ tsp/2.5g ground saffron

½ tsp/2.5g ground cardamom

1 tsp/5g salt

⅔ cup/6½ oz/210 g basmati rice, well washed

4 cups/1¾ pints/1 l chicken broth

2 tbsp yellow raisins

2 tbsp/2 oz/60 g chopped cashew nuts, roasted

Method

1. Cut each chicken thigh into 4 pieces. Heat the oil in a large, heavy-based frying pan and add the chili peppers, onion, ginger, garlic, spices, and a good pinch of salt. Fry over a low heat for 5 minutes or until the peppers and onion have softened.

2. Add the chicken and 2 tbsp of the yogurt. Increase the heat to medium and cook for 4 minutes or until the yogurt is absorbed. Repeat with the rest of the yogurt.

3. Increase the heat to high, stir in the tomatoes and 1 scant cup/7fl oz/200ml of water, and bring to the boil.

Reduce the heat, cover, and simmer for 30 minutes or until the chicken is tender, stirring occasionally, and adding more water if the sauce becomes too dry.

4. Uncover the pan, increase the heat to high and cook, stirring constantly, for 5 minutes or until the sauce thickens. Garnish with fresh coriander sprigs.

Chicken Rogan Josh

Ingredients

8 skinless boneless chicken thighs

1 tbsp vegetable oil

1 small red chili pepper and 1 small green chili pepper, seeded and thinly sliced

1 onion, thinly sliced

2in/5cm piece of fresh root ginger, finely chopped

2 cloves garlic, crushed

2 tbsp/30ml garam masala

1 tsp each paprika, turmeric, and chili powder

4 cardamom pods, crushed

salt

1 scant cup/7fl oz/200ml thick, plain yogurt

1¾ cups/14oz/400g canned chopped tomatoes

Fresh coriander (cilantro) leaves to garnish

Method

Cut the lamb from the bone into 1½in/4cm cubes. Season with salt and pepper.
Heat ghee in a large, heavy-based saucepan, add one-third of the lamb, and brown
well on all sides. Remove and brown the remainder in 2 batches. Remove and
reserve.

Add the onion and garlic to the pan juices and sauté for five minutes. Add the curry
paste and spices and cook for two minutes. Add the flour, stir well to combine and
add the chicken broth, all at once. Cook, stirring, until it starts to bubble, then add
the rest of the ingredients, and return the lamb to the pot. Cover and simmer
for 30 minutes or until the lamb is tender and cooked through.

Ingredients

1½ kg shoulder of lamb

salt and freshly ground black pepper

2 tbsp/50g ghee

1 Bermuda onion, finely chopped

1 clove garlic, finely chopped

1 tbsp/15g curry paste

¼ tsp/1.25g ground ginger

Lamb Korma

¼ tsp/1.25g turmeric

pinch of cayenne pepper

2 tbsp/30g all-purpose flour

1¼ cups/10 fl oz/300ml chicken broth

¾ cup/150g yellow raisins

⅔ cup/5fl oz/150ml yogurt

1 tbsp15ml lemon juice

Indian

55

Method

Trim the beans to lengths of 3in/8cm and discard any discolored tips. Peel the ginger and cut into fine matchstick (julienne) strips.

Heat a wok and add the vegetable and sesame oils. When hot, add the mustard seeds. Allow them to cook until they start popping. Add the ginger and cook for a further minute. Add the ground cumin, turmeric, and chili and stir until fragrant, 2 minutes.

Add all the beans and toss in the flavored oil to coat them thoroughly. Add the broth, cover and simmer for 5-8 minutes or until the liquid has almost evaporated completely, and the beans are tender.

Remove the lid and add the lemon juice, coriander and salt to taste. Stir thoroughly to combine all the ingredients then cool. Serve garnished with roasted chopped peanuts and, if desired, lemon wedges.

Green Bean Salad with Coriander and Ginger

Ingredients

1½ lb/700g fresh snake (long) beans

¾in/2cm piece fresh ginger

1 tbsp/15ml vegetable oil

1 tbsp/15ml sesame oil

1 tsp/5g mustard seeds

2 tsp/10g ground cumin

½ tsp turmeric

1 fresh green chili pepper, finely chopped

⅔ cup/5oz/150ml chicken/vegetable broth

2 lemons, juice squeezed

1 cup/4oz/125g fresh coriander (cilantro), washed, dried and chopped

salt to taste

⅓ cup/3oz/80g peanuts, roasted and chopped

Method

1. Put lamb cubes in a saucepan. Tie cloves, peppercorns, cardamom pods, cumin seeds, cinnamon, coriander seeds and chilies in a piece of cheesecloth and add to the pan with the measured water.

2. Bring to the boil, lower the heat, and simmer for 40 minutes or until meat is very tender. Strain, reserving lamb cubes and broth. Discard the spice bag.

3. Heat ghee or oil in a large frying pan, add onion, ginger, and garlic, and fry for 2 minutes, stirring frequently.

4. Add lamb cubes, stirring to coat them in the spices. Cook for 10 minutes, until golden-brown.

5. Meanwhile, drain rice and transfer to a large saucepan. Pour in enough of the reserved broth to cover the rice by about 1½in/4cm. Add the salt. Bring to the boil, cover, lower the heat, and cook for 10–15 minutes or until rice is almost tender and most of the broth has been absorbed.

6. Add rice to meat mixture in pan; fork through lightly. Cover tightly and cook over very low heat until rice is tender, adding more broth if necessary. Garnish with lemon wedges and serve with yogurt.

Ingredients

1 lb/500g lean boneless leg lamb, cubed

6 cloves

8 black peppercorns

4 green cardamom pods

1 tsp/5g cumin seeds

1in/2½cm cinnamon stick

1 tbsp/15g coriander seeds

2 small red chili peppers

5 cups/2 pints/1.2 l water

2 tbsp/30ml ghee or oil (page 40)

1 onion, minced

2 tbsp/30g grated fresh root ginger

2 cloves garlic, crushed

Lamb Pilau with Yogurt

2 cups/1 lb/500g basmati rice, soaked for

30 minutes in water to cover

½ tsp/2.5g salt

lemon wedges to garnish

yogurt to serve

Method

1. Place the tomatoes in a bowl, cover with boiling water, and leave to stand for 30 seconds. Skin the tomatoes, then finely dice the flesh.

2. Crush the cardamom seeds, using a pestle and mortar. Add the coriander, cumin, cinnamon, chili powder, turmeric, and 2 tbsp of water and mix to a paste. Set aside.

3. Heat the oil in a large, heavy-based saucepan. Fry the onion, garlic, and ginger for 3 minutes or until softened. Add the spice paste, mix well, and fry for 1 minute, stirring constantly.

4. Pour in the coconut milk and bring to the boil, stirring. Reduce the heat and simmer for 10 minutes or until the liquid has reduced slightly. Add the fish, tomatoes, and salt to taste. Partly cover the pan and simmer for a further 10 minutes or until the fish is cooked through, stirring occasionally. Garnish with coriander sprigs to serve.

Goan-Style Fish and Coconut Curry

Ingredients

2 ripe beefsteak tomatoes

2 cardamom pods, husks discarded
and seeds reserved

1 tsp/5g each of ground coriander, cumin,
cinnamon, and hot chili powder

½ tsp/2.5g ground turmeric

2 tbsp/30ml vegetable oil

1 onion, finely chopped

1 clove garlic, minced

1in/2.5cm piece fresh root ginger,
finely chopped

1¾ cups/14fl oz/400ml canned coconut milk

1lb/8oz/675g skinless white fish fillet, such as
snapper or cod, cut into 1in/2.5cm chunks

salt

Fresh coriander sprigs to garnish

Method:

1. Wash lentils in cold water.

2. Place lentils, water, turmeric, and garlic in a large saucepan and bring to the boil. Reduce the heat, cover, and simmer, stirring occasionally, for 30 minutes or until lentils are cooked. Remove cover from pan, bring to the boil, and boil to reduce the liquid by at least half.

3. Melt ghee or butter in a large frying pan, add onion, and cook for 5 minutes or until onion is soft. Stir in garam masala, ginger, coriander, and cayenne pepper and cook for 1 minute. Stir spice mixture into lentils and serve immediately.

Indian Dahl

Ingredients

1 cup/8oz/250g brown or red lentils

4 cups/1¾ pints/1 l water

1 tsp/5g ground turmeric

1 clove garlic, crushed

2 tbsp/1 fl oz/30ml ghee or clarified butter

1 large onion, chopped

1 tsp/5g garam masala

½ tsp/2.5g ground ginger

1 tsp/5g ground coriander

½ tsp/2.5g cayenne pepper

Method

Trim meat of all visible fat and set aside

To make marinade, combine yogurt, ginger, garlic, chili, cumin, cardamom, coriander, and food coloring. Blend tamarind paste with water and fold into yogurt mixture.

Rub marinade into meat and set aside, covered, for at least 3 hours or overnight.

Remove meat from marinade and brush with oil. Broil or barbecue over medium heat for 8–10 minutes, turning and basting frequently with marinade.

Ingredients

8 beef spare ribs

2 tbsp/30ml peanut oil

Marinade:

1 cup/8oz/250g plain yogurt

1½ tsp/7.5g grated fresh ginger

2 cloves garlic, crushed

3 tsp/15ml Tabasco

Tandoori Beef Ribs

1 tsp/5g ground cumin

1 tsp/5g ground cardamom

1 tbsp/15g finely chopped fresh coriander (cilantro)

few drops red food coloring

1 tbsp/15g tamarind paste

½ cup/4fl oz/125ml water

Method

1. Combine the lamb, 1 tbsp/15ml of the yogurt, the ginger, chili, 2 tbsp/30g of the chopped coriander, the cumin and ground coriander, and season. Shape the mixture into 16 balls.

2. Heat 1 tbsp/15ml of the oil in a large saucepan. Fry the meatballs for 10 minutes, turning until browned (you may have to cook them in batches). Drain on kitchen paper and set aside.

3. Heat the remaining oil in the pan. Add the onion and garlic and fry for 5 minutes or until softened, stirring occasionally. Mix the turmeric and garam masala with 1 tbsp/15ml water, then add to the onion and garlic. Add the remaining yogurt, 1 tbsp/15ml at a time, stirring well each time.

4. Add the tomatoes, meatballs and ⅔ cup/6½ fl oz/150ml of water to the mixture and bring to the boil. Partly cover the pan, reduce the heat and simmer for 30 minutes, stirring occasionally. Sprinkle over the rest of the coriander to garnish.

Indian Meatballs in Tomato Sauce

Ingredients

1lb/2oz/500g lean ground lamb	salt and black pepper
5 tbsp/90ml plain yogurt	2 tbsp/30ml vegetable oil
2in/5cm piece fresh root ginger, finely chopped	1 onion, chopped
1 green chili pepper, deseeded and finely chopped	2 cloves garlic, chopped
3 tbsp/45g chopped fresh coriander	½ tsp/2.5g turmeric
2 tsp/10g ground cumin	1 tsp/5g garam masala
2 tsp/10g ground coriander	1¾ cups/14 oz/400g can chopped tomatoes

Method

1. Heat the oil in a flameproof casserole dish or a large, heavy-based saucepan. Fry the onions, garlic, ginger, cinnamon, cloves, and cardamom for 5 minutes to soften the onions and garlic, and to release the flavors of the spices.

2. Add the lamb and fry for 5 minutes, turning, until it begins to color. Mix in the cumin and coriander, then add the yogurt, 1 tbsp/15ml at a time, stirring well after each addition.

3. Mix together the tomato paste and the broth and add to the lamb. Season to taste. Bring to the boil, then reduce the heat, cover, and simmer for 30 minutes or until the lamb is tender.

4. Stir in the spinach, cover, and simmer for another 15 minutes or until the mixture has reduced. Remove the cinnamon stick and the cardamom pods and mix in the almonds.

Lamb and Spinach Curry

Ingredients

2 tbsp/30ml vegetable oil

2 onions, minced

2 cloves garlic, minced

1in/2.5cm piece fresh root ginger, finely chopped

1 cinnamon stick

1 tsp ground cloves

3 cardamom pods

1lb/5oz/600g diced lamb

1 tbsp/15g ground cumin

1 tbsp/15g ground coriander

¼ cup/4 tbsp/60ml plain yogurt

2 tbsp/30ml tomato paste

1 scant cup/7fl oz/200ml beef broth

salt and black pepper

5 cups/1¼ lb/500g bags fresh spinach, finely chopped

2 tbsp/30g roasted flaked almonds

Method

1. Rinse chickens inside and out and pat dry with paper towels. Make deep gashes in thighs and on each side of breast. Pin back the wings.

2. Combine tandoori curry paste, yogurt, lemon juice, and melted butter. Place chickens in a stainless steel or other non-reactive bowl and spread the mixture all over, rubbing well into the gashes. Cover and refrigerate for 12 or more hours. Place chickens on a roasting rack in a baking dish and spoon any remaining marinade over chickens.

3. Preheat the oven to 370°F/190°C and cook for 1 hour. Baste with pan juices during cooking. When cooked, cover with foil and rest for 10 minutes before serving. Arrange crisp lettuce leaves on a large serving platter and cover with onion rings. Cut chicken into portions and place on the platter. Garnish with tomato wedges and lemon slices.

Ingredients

2 x 2lb/1 kg roasting chickens

3 tbsp/45ml tandoori curry paste

1 scant cup/7oz/200g plain yogurt

2 tbsp/30ml lemon juice

2 tbsp/30g melted butter

lettuce, onion rings, tomato and lemon for serving

Tandoori Chicken

Tip

Chickens portions may be used instead
of whole chickens. Turn frequently while
they are roasting.

Indian

Method

1. Place flour in a strong plastic bag and season with salt and pepper. Add cubed chuck steak, close bag, and shake until evenly coated.

2. Heat ghee or oil in a heavy-bottomed pan, add floured beef cubes, and fry for 5 minutes, stirring and turning meat so that all sides are browned.

3. Add onions and cook, stirring occasionally, for 5 minutes longer.

4. Stir in spices and cook for 3 minutes, then add garlic. Cook for 2 minutes.

5. Add measured hot water. Bring to the boil and boil briskly, stirring, for 5 minutes.

6. Stir in raisins and add more water, if necessary, to cover meat. Bring to the boil, lower the heat and simmer for 2¼ hours, adding more water as required. Serve at once or cool swiftly, chill and reheat next day.

Madras Curry

Ingredients

2 tbsp/1oz/30g flour

salt

freshly ground black pepper

1 lb/500g lean chuck steak, cubed

2oz/60g ghee or 4 tbsp oil

2 onions, minced

1 tsp/5g ground turmeric

1 tsp/5g ground coriander

1 tsp/5g cayenne pepper

½ tsp/2.5g ground black mustard seeds

½ tsp/2.5g ground cumin

2 cloves garlic, crushed

⅔ cup/5fl oz/155ml hot water

2 tbsp/2oz/60g seedless raisins

Method

1. Heat oil in a saucepan over a medium heat, add duck and cook, turning frequently, for 10 minutes or until brown on all sides. Remove and drain on absorbent kitchen paper.

2. Add onion, chopped red chili peppers, and lemongrass to pan and cook, stirring, for 3 minutes or until onion is golden. Stir in masala paste and cook for 2 minutes longer or until fragrant.

4. Stir in coconut milk, curry leaves, lime juice, and sugar and return duck to pan. Bring to the boil, reduce the heat, and simmer, stirring occasionally, for 45 minutes.

5. Add coriander, basil, and sliced green and red chili peppers and cook for 10 minutes longer or until duck is tender.

Masala Duck Curry

Ingredients

1 tbsp/15ml sesame oil

1 x 4 lb/2kg duck, cleaned and cut into 8 pieces

1 onion, chopped

2 small fresh red chili peppers, finely chopped

1 stalk fresh lemongrass, finely chopped

or ½ tsp/2.5g dried lemon grass, soaked

in hot water until soft

2 tbsp/30ml green masala curry paste

1½ cups/12fl oz/375ml coconut milk

3 fresh or dried curry leaves

1 tbsp/25ml lime juice

1 tbsp/15g brown sugar or piloncillo

1 tbsp/15g chopped fresh coriander (cilantro)

1oz/30g fresh basil leaves

3 fresh green chili peppers, seeded and sliced

2 fresh red chili peppers, seeded and sliced

Method

Place beansprouts, cucumbers, coconut, tomatoes, coriander, mint, basil, green onions (scallions), lemon juice in a bowl. Season to taste with salt and pepper and toss to combine. Cover and stand at room temperature for 2–3 hours before serving.

Mogul Salad

Ingredients

1 scant cup/6½oz/200g mung beansprouts

3 cucumbers, diced

4 tsp/20g grated fresh or shredded coconut

2 tomatoes, diced

½ cup/2oz/50g chopped coriander, leaves

½ cup/2oz/50g fresh chopped mint leaves

½ cup/2oz/50g fresh chopped basil leaves

1 bunch/125g/4oz green onions (scallions), chopped

2 tbsp/50ml lemon juice

salt

freshly ground black pepper

Method

1. For the marinade, grind the salt, garlic, ginger, coriander, mint, turmeric, chili powder, and cardamom seeds to a paste, using a pestle and mortar or a coffee grinder. Transfer to a large, non-metallic bowl, stir in the yogurt and lemon juice, and mix together well.

2. Score each chicken breast 4 times with a sharp knife, then add to the bowl and turn to coat thoroughly. Cover and chill for 6 hours, or overnight.

3. Preheat the oven to 425°F/220°C. Place the chicken breasts on a rack in a roasting pan and cook for 20-25 minutes, or until they are tender and the juices run clear when pierced with a skewer.

Roasted Tandoori Chicken Breasts

Ingredients

4 skinless boneless chicken breasts

For the marinade

1 tsp/5g salt

2 cloves garlic, chopped

1in/2.5cm piece fresh root ginger, chopped

1 tbsp/15g chopped fresh coriander (cilantro), plus extra leaves to garnish

1 tbsp chopped fresh mint

½ tsp/2.5g ground turmeric

½ tsp/2.5g hot chili powder

2 cardamom pods, split, husks discarded and seeds reserved

4 tbsp/2fl oz/50ml plain yogurt

½ lemon, juice squeezed

Method

1. To make marinade, place garlic, ginger, chili peppers, lemon juice, sugar, and salt to taste in a bowl and mix to combine. Add shrimp and toss to coat with marinade. Cover and marinate in the refrigerator for 15–20 hours.

2. Place tomatoes in a food processor or blender and process until smooth.

3. Pre-heat oven to 325°F/160°C. Heat oil in a wok or large frying pan, reduce heat to low, add shrimp and marinade and cook, stirring constantly, for 2–3 minutes. Transfer shrimp to an ovenproof dish, add tomatoes and coriander and mix well to combine. Bake for 20 minutes.

Spicy Red Shrimp

Ingredients

16 large raw shrimp, shelled and deveined

3 large tomatoes, peeled, seeded and chopped

1 tbsp/15ml vegetable oil

1 small bunch coriander, leaves removed and chopped

Marinade:

6 cloves garlic, minced

2 tsp/10g finely chopped fresh ginger

8 red or green chili peppers, finely chopped

3 tbsp/45ml lemon juice

1 tbsp/15g superfine (caster) sugar

salt

Method

1. Pierce fish strips several times with a fork and place in a shallow glass or ceramic bowl.

2. To make marinade, place onion, garlic, ginger, cumin, garam masala, cardamom, turmeric, chili powder, coriander, and tomato paste in a food processor or blender and process until smooth. Add yogurt and mix to combine. Spoon marinade over fish, toss to combine, cover, and marinate in the refrigerator for 3 hours.

3. Preheat barbecue to a medium heat. Drain fish and thread onto lightly oiled skewers. Place skewers on lightly oiled barbecue grill and cook, turning several times, for 5–6 minutes or until fish is cooked.

4. To make raitha, place cucumber, mint, and yogurt in a bowl and mix to combine. Serve skewers with lemon wedges and raitha.

Ingredients

1½ lb/750g firm white fish fillets, cut into ¾in/2cm wide strips

1 lemon, cut into wedges

Spicy yogurt marinade

1 onion, minced

4 cloves garlic, crushed

2 tsp/10g finely grated fresh ginger

1 tbsp/15g ground cumin

1 tbsp/15g garam masala

3 cardamom pods, crushed

1 tsp/5g ground turmeric

2 tsp/10g chili powder

2 tsp/10g ground coriander

1 tbsp/15ml tomato paste

1¾ cups/11oz/350g plain yogurt

Cucumber raitha

1 small cucumber, finely chopped

1 tbsp/15g chopped fresh mint

1 scant cup/7 fl oz/200g plain yogurt

Tikka Fish Kabobs

Note:

When buying fish fillets, look for those that

are shiny and firm with a pleasant sea smell.

Avoid those that are dull, soft, discolored, or

oozing water when touched.

Method

1. Rinse the lentils and drain well, then place in a large saucepan with 3¾ cups/1½ pints/850ml of water. Bring to the boil, skimming off any scum, then stir in the turmeric. Reduce the heat and partly cover the pan. Simmer for 30–35 minutes, until thickened, stirring occasionally.

2. Heat the oil in a small frying pan, then add the ginger and cumin seeds, and fry for 30 seconds or until the cumin seeds start to pop. Stir in the ground coriander and fry for 1 minute.

3. Season the lentils with plenty of salt and pepper, then add the toasted spices. Stir in the chopped coriander, mixing well. Transfer to a serving dish and garnish with the paprika and coriander leaves.

Split Lentil Dahl with Ginger and Coriander

Ingredients

1 cup/7oz/200g dried split red lentils

½ tsp/2.5g turmeric

1 tbsp/15ml vegetable oil

½in/1cm piece fresh root ginger, finely chopped

1 tsp/5g cumin seeds

1 tsp/5g ground coriander

salt and black pepper

4 tbsp/60g chopped fresh coriander, plus extra leaves to garnish

½ tsp/2.5g paprika to garnish

Method

1. Heat oil in a saucepan over a medium heat, stir in masala paste and chili powder. Cook for 2 minutes. Add ginger, garlic, and onion and cook, stirring, for 3 minutes or until onion is soft. Add cauliflower, beans, eggplant (aubergines), carrots, and mushrooms and cook, stirring, for 5 minutes.

2. Stir in tomatoes and broth and bring to boil. Reduce heat and simmer, stirring occasionally, for 20 minutes or until vegetables are tender.

Vegetable Korma

Ingredients

2 tbsp/20ml vegetable oil

2 tbsp/30ml green masala paste

1 tsp/5g chili powder

1 tbsp/15g finely grated fresh ginger

2 cloves garlic, crushed

1 onion, chopped

1 lb/500g cauliflower, cut into flowerets

¾ cup/6oz/185g green beans

3 baby eggplant (aubergines)

2 carrots, sliced

1 cup/4oz/125g button mushrooms

1¾ cups/14oz/440g canned tomatoes, undrained and mashed

1 cup/8fl oz/250ml vegetable broth

Method

1. Trim meat of all visible fat and set aside.

2. To make marinade, combine yogurt, ginger, garlic, lime juice, cumin, cardamom, chili powder, and garam masala. Add enough red food coloring to turn the marinade pink. Add cutlets, toss to coat, and set aside to marinate for 30 minutes.

3. Remove cutlets from marinade. Broil or barbecue for 6–8 minutes, turning frequently and basting with marinade.

Ingredients

8 lamb cutlets

Marinade

4 tbsp/60ml plain yogurt

1 tsp/5g grated fresh ginger

1 clove garlic, crushed

1 tbsp/15ml lime juice

1 tsp/5g ground cumin

¼ tsp/1.25g ground cardamom

¼ tsp/1.25g chili powder

¼ tsp/1.25g garam masala

few drops red food coloring

Tandoori Lamb Cutlets

Tandoori is a favorite Indian way of cooking.
Traditionally the food is cooked in a vat-shaped
clay oven called a tandoor. This recipe uses the
traditional spices and flavorings of the tandoori
but the cutlets are broiled or barbecued.

Indian

Method

1. Preheat the oven to 300°F/150°C. Place the rice, milk, and evaporated milk in a small, heavy-based saucepan and bring to a simmer, taking care not to let the mixture boil. Cook, uncovered, for 10 minutes.

2. Butter an ovenproof dish. Transfer the rice mixture to the dish, then stir in the cardamom seeds, cinnamon, sugar, almonds and pistachios, reserving 1 tbsp/15g to garnish. Bake for 2 hours, or until reduced to a thick consistency, stirring in the skin that forms on top every 30 minutes. Remove the cinnamon stick. Serve warm or cold, garnished with the reserved pistachios.

Indian Rice Pudding with Pistachios

Ingredients

2oz/50g basmati (long-grain) rice

2 cups/¾ pint/425ml full-fat milk

1¾ cups/14 fl oz/400ml canned full-cream evaporated milk

Butter for greasing

3 cardamom pods, seeds only

1 cinnamon stick

2 tbsp/2oz/50g superfine (caster) sugar

2 tbsp/30g toasted flaked almonds

2 tbsp/1oz/25g shelled pistachios, roughly chopped

Method

1. To make the jellebi batter, sift flour and salt into a large bowl, make a well in the center, and add yogurt. Stir, gradually incorporating surrounding flour to make a smooth liquid batter. Stir in sugar and yeast, cover, and set aside in a warm place for 4–6 hours, or until batter is spongy.

2. Make the syrup. Put sugar and measured water in a heavy-based saucepan. Stir over gentle heat until sugar has dissolved, then add cinnamon, cardamom pods, and cloves. Increase the heat and boil rapidly until the syrup is thick and heavy and has reduced by half. Reduce heat to lowest setting to keep syrup warm while cooking jallebi.

3. Heat the oil for deep frying. Fill a large piping bag fitted with a narrow nozzle with the jallebi batter. Squeeze the batter in spirals into the hot oil, stopping the flow when each jallebi measures about 4in/10cm across. Do not cook too many jallebi at the same time or the oil will cool and they will be soggy. Remove them with a slotted spoon as soon as they are golden-brown.

4. Drain jallebi on paper towels, then transfer to the pan of hot syrup. Dip for up to 5 minutes, depending on how sweet you like your jallebi. Drain off excess syrup and serve.

Jallebi are deep-fried spirals of cooked sweet batter which are dunked – or soaked – in a sweet spicy syrup.

Ingredients

4 cups/1 lb/250g all-purpose (plain) flour

½ tsp/2.5g salt

1 cup/8fl oz/250ml plain yogurt

2 tsp/10g sugar

1 package active dry yeast

oil for deep frying

Syrup:

2½ cups/1¼ lb/500g soft light brown sugar

4 cups/1¾ pints/1 l water

1 cinnamon stick, broken into short lengths

8 green cardamom pods

4–6 cloves

Jallebi

Tip

Jallebi are deep-fried spirals

of cooked sweet yeast dough

which are dunked or soaked

in a sweet spicy syrup.

Indian

Method

1. Put ⅔ cup/5oz/155g of the sugar with the measured water in a wide saucepan or deep frying pan. Stir over gentle heat until sugar has dissolved, then add cardamom pods, increase the heat, and boil for 15 minutes to make a light syrup. Reduce heat to lowest setting to keep syrup warm.

2. Combine flour and powdered milk in a bowl. Rub in ghee or butter, then add remaining sugar, cream cheese, rosewater, and enough milk or yogurt (about 2 tbsp/30ml) to form a soft dough. Knead lightly and roll into 18 small balls.

3. Heat oil for deep frying. Cook jamuns in small batches, keeping them moving in the oil until they are golden-brown all over.

4. Remove jamuns with a slotted spoon and drain on paper towels for 5 minutes. Remove syrup from heat and carefully add jamuns. Allow to cool to room temperature in syrup. To serve, transfer jamuns to individual plates with a slotted spoon, then add 2–3 tbsp/30-45ml syrup.

Tip

These small dumplings in a spicy syrup are a traditional dessert. They are usually made with full fat powdered milk. This is not always easy to obtain, so this recipe uses skimmed milk powder and adds cream cheese.

Gulab Jamun

Ingredients

¾ cup/6oz/175g sugar

2½ cups/1 pints/600ml water

8 green cardamom pods

2 tbsp/1oz/30g self-rising flour

½ cup/4oz/125g powdered skimmed milk

2 tbsp/1oz/30g ghee or butter

2 tbsp/1oz/30g cream cheese

1–2 tbsp/15-30ml rosewater

milk or plain low-fat yogurt

oil for deep frying

Index